How We Make Music

Roland Graham

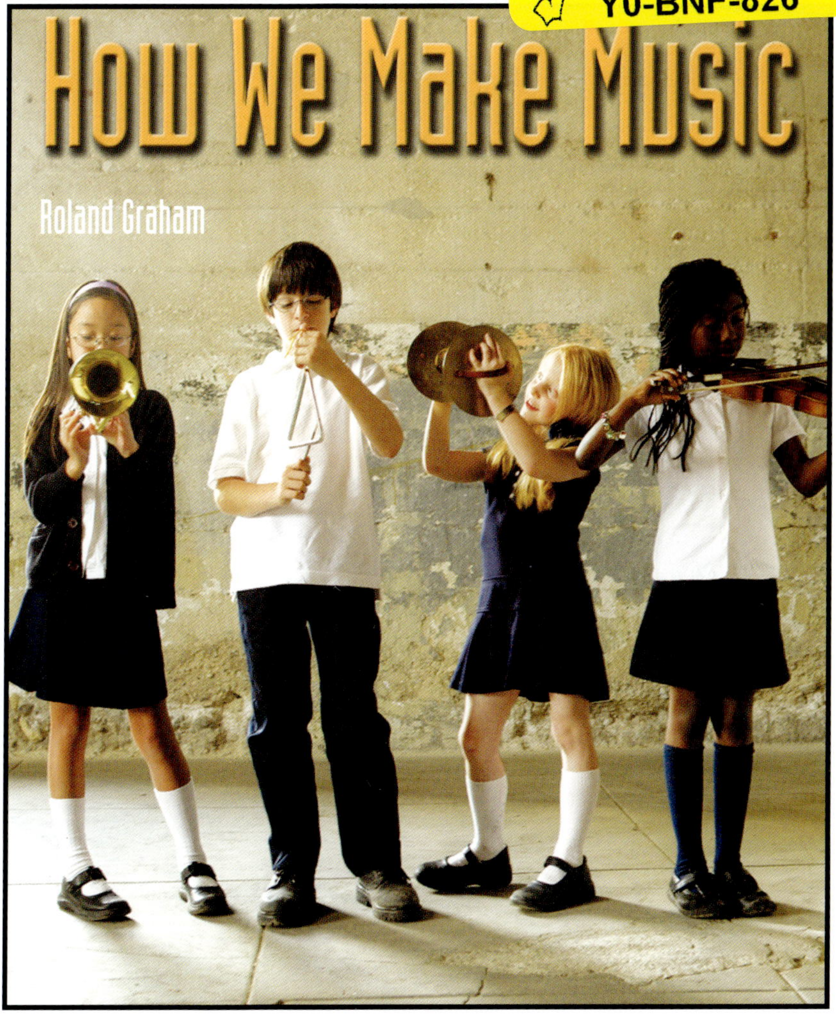

Rosen Classroom Books & Materials
New York

You can sing to make music.

You can make music with your hands and feet.

You play drums by hitting them with sticks or your hands.

Big drums make low sounds.

Small drums make high sounds.

You play the recorder by blowing into it.

You can make different sounds by covering the holes with your fingers.

You play the guitar by plucking the strings with your fingers.

Thick strings make low sounds.
Thin strings make high sounds.

You play the piano by pressing the keys with your fingers.

The keys on the left make low sounds. The keys on the right make high sounds.

Words to Know

drums

guitar

keys

piano

recorder

strings